Inspirational Poems and Encouragement for Everyone

KATHLEEN GODWIN

authorHOUSE

AuthorHouse™
1663 Liberty Drive
Bloomington, IN 47403
www.authorhouse.com
Phone: 833-262-8899

Published by AuthorHouse   04/28/2021

ISBN: 978-1-6655-2432-2 (sc)
ISBN: 978-1-6655-2431-5 (hc)
ISBN: 978-1-6655-2430-8 (e)

Library of Congress Control Number: 2021908522

Print information available on the last page.

This book is printed on acid-free paper.

Contents

Acknowledgments

First of all is my Savior, Jesus Christ, who is the head of my life. He inspired me to write the messages within these poems, to share love, joy, peace, faith, hope, and kindness to everyone in the United States of America and around the world.

To my husband, Darryl Godwin Sr.: God has blessed us in marriage since November 3, 1990. Thank you for your love and support with words of encouragement so that I can continue to write inspirational and encouraging poems. God has blessed us with two wonderful children.

To our children, Ericka Godwin and Darryl Godwin Jr., who are blessings and gifts from God: Thank you for your love, support, and kind words for me to share God's words of inspiration and encouragement for everyone in the United States of America and around the world. Remember, Ericka and Darryl, always to put God first in your lives, and God will bless you to become successful.

Special thanks to AuthorHouse for your love and support in making my poems into a book of words of inspiration and encouragement for everyone to use for themselves and to share with each other. I appreciate your team of editors, publishing consultants, and everyone at your company for their hard work. Thank you, AuthorHouse, for publishing my poems so that I can share God's words of love, joy, peace, hope, faith, and kindness with everyone. I hope and pray that everyone can share these same words with each other in the United States of America and around the world.

To everyone who takes time to read these poems of inspiration and encouragement: I appreciate everyone's love and support. I hope and pray that these words of love, joy, peace, hope, faith, and kindness become showers of blessings for everyone. Everyone can share these same words with each other in the United States of America and around the world.

Walking on the Streets of Gold

As I walk on the streets of gold,
First I want to seek King Jesus
And give him the praise.
As I continue my journey on the
Streets of gold, I want to give
Thanks to God for freeing me from
All the troubles of this world
And freeing my body from all pain.
As I keep walking on the streets
Of gold, I want to find my loved ones
Who have already entered the streets
Of gold before me and give them my love.
I want to let my loved ones know that
I love them, and they were truly missed on
The earth below.
Although my family may be apart, some are
Here above the clouds, and some are
On the earth below the clouds, but all my family
Members will be in my heart.
I will continue my journey, and
I will not quit until that great day
When everyone on earth below the clouds
Unites with everyone here on the
Streets of gold, and we are reunited
As one family
As I walk on the streets of gold.

Walking through the Grocery Store

As I was walking through the grocery store, I was
Pushing a grocery cart so that I could place two loaves of
Bread into my grocery cart in order to purchase them. Also,
I needed to make a beef stew, and I
needed to purchase one pound of
Beef along with these vegetables: green
peas, carrots, tomatoes, and corn.

First, I was walking with my grocery cart into the bakery,
Where I was greeted by a wonderful salesperson who had a
Smile on her face. She said to me, "Can
I help you with some bread
Today?" Then I said to the bakery
salesperson: "Yes, I would like
Two loaves of bread to go along with my beef stew."
After the bakery salesperson gave me two loaves of bread,
I said to her, "Thank you, and have a nice day."

Next, I was walking and pushing my
grocery cart through the aisle of
Canned vegetables, where I could find
cans of vegetables that are
Easy to reach, such as cans of green
peas, carrots, and tomatoes.
Therefore, I placed some of these vegetable cans into my
Grocery cart. Yet not only was the can of corn on
The top shelf, it was beyond my reach.

Since I was unable to reach the can of corn, I asked a nice
Salesperson who was standing alongside me if he could
Reach the can of corn for me. He greeted me with a smile as
He placed the can of corn in my hands. After I placed the
Can of corn into my grocery cart, I said to him,
"Thank you for your kindness, and have a nice day."

My next journey was to the aisle of
meat, where I as greeted with
A smile from a kind butcher who said
to me, "Can I help you with
Some meat today?" And then I said to him,
"Yes, my beef stew will not be complete
without some beef. I need
One pound of beef." After I placed
the one pound of beef into
My grocery cart, I said to him, "Thank
you, and have a nice day."
My grocery cart was full of many
ingredients to make my beef stew,
And so I proceeded toward the cashier, who
was standing at the checkout line.
While I was emptying out my grocery cart,
the good cashier greeted me with
A smile and said to me, "Did you find everything that
You want today in this grocery store?" Then I said to her,
"Yes, I found the most important ingredient
for my beef stew today—
The best ingredient is kindness.
I found kindness from four wonderful salespersons:
A wonderful salesperson in the bakery
aisle, a nice salesperson in the

Canned vegetable aisle, a kind butcher
in the meat aisle, and a
Good cashier in this checkout line."

After the cashier rang up the total
cost of the kindness from all
Four salespersons, she said to me, "Your total sum for
Kindness is free."

Kindness can never be bought because
kindness is always free.

Time Does Not Wait

As the years pass, we realize that
Our age is a number that will always increase when
We travel on our life's journey-road. Also, we know that
We must travel together as we move forward to our
Destiny. Yet we cannot take any detours, and we cannot
Take any shortcuts to slow down time because
Time constantly moves forward.

We understand that we must make a few stops
Along our pathway so that we can enjoy the phenomenal
Materials that nature provides for us. Therefore,
We can take a deep breath so that we can smell the
Sweet flowers deep in the valley between the mountains.

We can visualize the wonderful peaks on top of
Mountains. In addition, we can listen to the
Sweet melody of the sound made by
the rushing waves of the
Ocean. Also, we can drink the natural spring water from the
Beautiful waterfalls. After we have enjoyed the
Wonderful materials of nature, then we must keep
Traveling on the road until we reach our destiny.

When we come to the end of our journey, and
We have reached our destiny, then we realize that
Our life's journey is short. Yet we are older in age at the
End of our journey than we were at the beginning of
Our life journey since time does not wait for us.

Our valuable lesson that we learned is that
We cannot turn back the hands of time, and we cannot
Push time forward. Time moves constantly forward at its
Own pace.

We must endure the beautiful moments
Together as we journey toward our life's destiny.

Keep Life Simple with a Brown Paper Bag

One ordinary day, I had a to-do list that was
Long, with six things for me to do, and I knew these
Things were going to turn my day into a very busy
Day. These are the six things: purchase food at the grocery
Store, mail a box at the post office, put a trash bag
Liner into a trash can, cover a book binder with a
Book cover, put a liner into my dresser drawer, and
Clean out my clothes closet.

I went to the grocery store, and I bought enough
Groceries to fill five brown paper bags. Also,
I reused these five brown paper bags in these five
Different ways:

I reused one brown paper bag as mailing paper to
Wrap a box, and I took the box to the post office to
Mail it.

I reused one brown paper bag as a trash bag liner for
My trash can so that it could be used to collect trash.

I reused one brown paper bag to cover the binder of
My book so that it could protect my book binder.

I reused one brown paper bag as a liner for my dresser
Drawer so that it could protect my clothes from the wood
Chips in my dresser drawer.

I reused one brown paper bag to put old clothes in
When I removed the old clothes from my clothes closet.

A lesson that I learned and want you to know is this:
When your daily to-do list is long with things that
Make your day very busy, remember to keep life
Simple with a brown paper bag.

Keep Life Simple with a Wooden Clothespin

One ordinary day I began my day with a to-do list that had
Five long things for me to do, and I knew that these
Things were going to keep my day very busy. These are the
Five things: Pin wet clothes onto a clothesline, pin a sleeveless
Tank top onto a clothes hanger, pin a grocery list onto my
Refrigerator door, pin family pictures onto a string, and
Pin a bag of opened potato chips.

First I washed twenty T-shirts, and I washed one sleeveless
Tank top in my washing machine. After these clothes had
Finished washing, then I used forty-two wooden clothespins to
Pin these wet clothes onto a clothesline outside to dry.

When I removed my dry clothes—twenty T-shirts and
One tank top—along with the forty-two
clothespins off the clothesline,
Then I was able to reuse all forty-two wooden clothespins.

I reused two wooden clothespins to pin my sleeveless tank
Top onto a clothes hanger so that I could hang it in my
Clothes closet.

I reused one of the wooden clothespins
with a magnet glued to it
So that I could pin my grocery list onto
my refrigerator door so that
I would know what items to purchase at the grocery store.

I reused thirty-eight wooden clothespins so that I could pin
Thirty-eight beautiful family pictures
onto a string that hung across
A wall in my house.

At the end of my long day, I reused one
of the wooden clothespins to
Tightly close a bag of potato chips so that the potato chips
Would not become stale.

The lesson that I learned and that I want
you to know is when your day is
Very busy with a long to-do list, then you
do not allow yourself to become
Stressed, but you find ways to simplify your day.

Remember, you keep your life simple
with a wooden clothespin.

When We Share Joy Together

When we rake pine needles and pine cones
Together in the fall, we share lots of
Smiles, love, and laughter. Also, we can rake together
Pine needles and pine cones off the ground that had
Fallen down from our pine trees.

Indeed, we enjoy painting our pine cones these
Colors: red, purple, yellow, and blue. We also enjoy
Pasting our colorful pine cones together so that
We can make our beautiful pine cone wreath that
We hang on our front door.

When we plant tomato plants in our garden,
We share lots of smiles, kindness, and laughter.
Indeed, we share love with our tomato plants because
We plant them in rich soil in the spring.

At the same time, we feed our tomato plants lots of
Water and fertilizer so that they can produce many
Red, delicious tomatoes in the summer.

In the summer we share happiness together because
We enjoy eating our red, delicious tomatoes.

When we plant together tulips in our garden,
We share lots of kindness, smiles, and laughter.
Indeed, we share love with our tulips in the
Fall, when we plant our tulip bulbs in rich soil
So that our tulip flowers can bloom in the spring.

In the spring we can enjoy picking tulips of
These colors: purple, yellow, red, and orange.

As the seasons change from fall to winter,
Winter to spring, and spring to summer with time,
Flowers and vegetables change their blooms
With time.

The lesson we have learned is that
The best time is when we spend time together and
When we share joy together.

Our Ladder of Success

When we climb our ladder of success together
With God, then we must climb five steps
So that we can reach the top step of success.

When we climb onto the first step of our ladder of
Success with God, then he gives us love to build a
Strong family foundation.

When we climb onto the second step of our ladder of
Success with God, then he gives us faith to help
Us build a strong religious foundation.

When we climb onto the third step of our ladder of
Success with God, then he gives us hope to help
Us build a strong educational foundation.

When we climb onto the fourth step of our ladder of
Success with God, then he gives us grace to help
Us build a strong job foundation.

When we climb onto the fifth step of our ladder of
Success with God, then he gives us joy to help
Us become successful in life.

When we have reached the
Top of our ladder of success, Then we can help others to
Succeed in life.

We can only reach the top of our ladder of success if
We take God with us, and we help others along the way
To become successful in life.

Strangers Are Unknown Friends

When you see strangers in need of food,
You can give food to strangers.

When strangers smile at you,
You can smile at strangers.

When you see strangers in need of clothes,
You can give clothes to strangers.

When you see strangers in need of happiness,
You can share words of encouragement
To strangers.

When you see strangers fall down to the streets,
You can help strangers to stand up.

Remember, strangers are unknown friends
Who are ready to become your friends.

Blessings in Your House Fire

When you lose your food in your house fire,
You will find friends who have kindness;
Friends will give you food.

When you lose your clothes in your house fire,
You will find friends who have love;
Friends will give you clothes.

When you lose your furniture in your house fire,
You will find friends who have joy;
Friends will give you furniture.

When you lose your appliances in your house fire,
You will find friends who have faith;
Friends will give you appliances.

So remember, your material things can be replaced
From your house fire; You will find blessings
Of kindness, love, joy and faith from friends.

You Are a Reflection of the World

When you smile at the world,
The world will smile at you.

When you give joy to the world,
The world will give joy to you.

When you give love to the world,
The world will give love to you.

When you give peace to the world,
The world will give peace to you.

When you give kindness to the world,
The world will give kindness to you.

Remember, if you want the world to give
You joy, love, peace and kindness,
You must give the world joy, love peace and
Kindness because you are a reflection of the world.

Two Heads Are Better than One

When trials in our lives are painful,
We put our heads together;
We find answers together to overcome our trials.

When challenges to our lives cause us to have depression,
We put our heads together;
We overcome depression together with love.

When storms in our lives create darkness,
We put our heads together;
We enjoy the rainbow and the sunshine together
After the storms.

When problems in our lives cause us to fall into pitfalls,
We use our strength together to climb out of our pitfalls.
Remember, if we want to overcome our problems in
Our life journeys together, then we must share our
Solutions because two heads are better than one.

High Self-Esteem

When you are exposed to your life's daily challenges with
Obstacles and stress, your good attitude will help
You to confront obstacles and stress.

When you believe in yourself, you can increase
Your confidence to reach higher goals.

When you have good patience with time,
You can endure life in different ways and with
Less stress.

When you have strong determination and inspiration,
You can increase your strength to confront
Your struggles.

You will learn that to overcome your obstacles
And challenges you must have high self-esteem.

Share Kindness with Your Neighbors

When your neighbors are hungry,
You share joy by giving food to
Your neighbors.

When your neighbors are sick,
You share love by praying for
Your neighbors.

When your neighbors are in need of clothes,
You share happiness by giving clothes
To your neighbors.

When your neighbors lose loved ones to death,
You share words of hope with your
Neighbors.

God loves you, and God wants you to love your
Neighbors as you love yourself.

Share Kindness with Your Mother

When you share a dinner with your mother,
You share love while eating dinner
With your mother.

When you share kind words with your mother,
You will receive words of wisdom from
Your mother.

When you help your mother to clean her house,
You share love while cleaning her house.

When you help your mother to cook,
You share joy while cooking food with
Your mother.

You become wise when you learn words of wisdom from
Your mother, when you share kindness
With your mother.

Give and You Will Receive

When you give love to your children,
You will receive love from your children.

When you give kindness to your children,
You will receive kindness from your children.

When you give joy to your children,
You will receive joy from your children.

When you give respect to your children,
You will receive respect from your children.

If you want your children to love you, then you must
Love your children.

Jesus loves you, and Jesus loves all the children of the world.

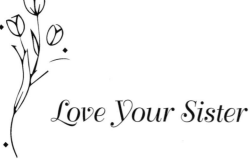

Love Your Sister

When you give love to your sister,
Your sister will give love to you.

When you give joy to your sister,
Your sister will give joy to you.

When you give words of encouragement to your sister,
Your sister will give words of encouragement to you.

When you help your sister in her time of need,
Your sister will help you in your time of Need.

God loves you, and God wants you to love your sister.

Love Your Brother

When your brother is in the need of food,
You share love by giving food to your brother.

When your brother is sick,
You share hope by praying for your brother.

When your brother is in the need of clothes,
You share joy by giving clothes to your brother.

When your brother has depression,
You share love by giving words of encouragement
To your brother.

God wants you to ask yourself this question:
Am I my brother's keeper?

Be a Good Samaritan

When poor people need food,
Be a good Samaritan with kindness;
You can give food to poor people.

When poor people need clothes,
Be a good Samaritan with love;
You can give clothes to poor people.

When poor people need wells for water,
Be a good Samaritan with joy;
You can help to dig wells for poor people.

When poor people are sick,
Be a good Samaritan with hope;
You can pray to God for the healing of poor people.

A lesson to learn for you: You are one of God's
Children, and God wants you to share your
Blessings of kindness, love, joy, and hope with
Poor people.

Keep Your Life Simple
with a Shoebox

When your family pictures are scattered about,
You can gather your family pictures.
You can keep your family pictures in a shoebox.

When you have some family jewelry that you treasure,
You can keep your family jewelry in your shoebox.

When your buttons fall off your clothes,
You can keep your buttons in your shoebox.

When You need to keep your coins in a safe box,
That needs neither a key nor a lock,
You can keep your coins in your shoebox.

You can keep your life simple with the small things in
Your shoebox.

The small things in life are the things that really count.
You should always thank God for the small things in your life.

Sister's Faith

Sister, keep faith in God.
When you begin your new job,
You have faith that God will bless you
To reach your goals.

Sister, keep faith in God.
When you buy your new house,
You have faith that God will bless you
To make your mortgage payments.

Sister, keep faith in God.
When you travel to cities,
You have faith that God will bless you to
Enjoy all the beautiful things in each city.

Sister, keep faith in God.
When you raise your daughter,
You have faith that God will bless you with
Wisdom to make the right choice between
Right and wrong.
You can pass the same wisdom
On to your daughter.
God loves you.

Brother's Faith

Brother, keep faith in God.
When you buy your new house,
You have faith that God will bless you to
Make your mortgage payments.

Brother, keep faith in God.
When you open your new business,
You have faith that God will bless you with
Love, joy, and kindness from people
Who will support your new business.

Brother, keep faith in God.
When you raise your son,
You have faith that God will bless you with
Wisdom to make the right choice
Between right and wrong.
You can pass
The same wisdom on to your son.

Remember, brother, to keep faith in God.
Nothing is impossible with God.
God loves you.

Mother's Faith

Mother, keep faith in God.
When you have raised your children,
You have faith that God will provide all
Their needs, and you can pray to God
To ask God to protect your children from all harm.

Mother, keep faith in God.
When you travel to cities,
You have faith that God will always be with you.
You can enjoy the wonderful things in each city.

Mother, keep faith in God.
When you begin your new job,
You have faith that God will bless you to learn
New skills so that you can reach your goals.

Mother, all your blessings come from God.
God loves you,
And
I love you.

Father's Faith

Father, keep faith in God.
When you retire from your job,
You have faith that God will bless you
With all your needs to enjoy your retirement.

Father, keep faith in God.
When you have sickness,
You have faith that God will bless you with
Strength to heal your body.

Father, keep faith in God.
When you have challenges in your life,
You have faith that God will help you to
Face your challenges because God is always with you.

Father, keep faith in God because God will never
Leave you or forsake you.
God loves you,
And
I love you.

Daughter's Faith

Daughter, keep faith in God.
When you begin your new job,
You have faith that God will bless you to
Become successful and reach your goals.

Daughter, keep faith in God.
When you travel around the world,
You have faith that God is always with you.
You can enjoy all the beautiful places of
This world and all the wonderful people.

Daughter, keep faith in God.
When you open your new business,
You have faith that God will bless you with
Love, joy, hope, and kindness from people.

Daughter, keep faith in God.
All your blessings come from God.
God loves you,
And
I love you.

Son's Faith

Son, keep faith in God.
When you begin your new job,
You have faith that God will bless you
With hope to become successful.

Son, keep faith in God.
When you buy your new house,
You have faith that God will bless you with
Love to make your mortgage payments.

Son, keep faith in God.
When you travel to new cities,
You have faith to know that God will always
Be with you so that you can enjoy all the
Wonderful things in each city.

Son, keep faith in God.
All your blessings come from God.
God loves you,
And
I love you.

A Child's Faith

When you teach a child about faith in God,
A child will have faith in God to learn
How to share joy with everyone.

When you teach a child about faith in God,
A child will have faith in God to learn
How to share love with everyone.

When you teach a child about faith in God,
A child will have faith in God to learn
How to share kindness with everyone.

When you teach a child about faith in God,
A child will have faith in God to learn
How to share peace with everyone.

The lesson learned is that a child can always
Have faith in God, and a child can always
Share joy, love, kindness, and peace with everyone.

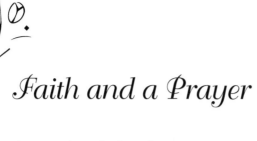

Faith and a Prayer

When you have faith and a prayer,
You will have faith that God will
Bless you with a home when you are
Homeless.

When you have faith and a prayer,
You will have faith, and you can
Pray that God will heal you from your sickness.

When you have faith and a prayer,
You will have faith that God will
Bless you with a Job when you are jobless.

When you have faith and a prayer,
You will have faith, and you can
Pray that God will bless you with strength
To overcome your challenges.

Remember, you are a child of God, and God
Will take care of you.

God's Phone Number Is Prayer

When you call God on your telephone,
You can dial P for pray; you can pray to
God any time of the day.

When you call God on your telephone,
You can dial R for ready; you can pray to God,
And God is always ready to listen to you.

When you call God on your telephone,
You can dial A for answer; you can pray to
God, and God will answer your prayers.

When you call God on your telephone,
You can dial Y for you; God loves you.

When you call God on your telephone,
You can dial E for everyone; you can pray
To God, and you can ask God to bless everyone.

When you call God on your telephone,
You can dial R for remember.
God wants you to remember that God's telephone line
Is always open, and you can always call God.
God's phone number is
PRAYER.

Jesus's News Reporter

You can become Jesus's news reporter
When you report about the good news of
Jesus feeding five thousand people with
Two fish and five loaves of bread.

You can become Jesus's news reporter
When you report about the good news of
Jesus giving eyesight to the blind people.

You can become Jesus's news reporter
When you report about the good news of
Jesus healing thousands of people.

You can become Jesus's news reporter
When you report the good news of
Jesus loving everyone.

The best way to spread the news is by word of mouth.
Spread the good news about Jesus.
Be Jesus's news reporter.

Everyday Kind Words

Thank you, God, for your kindness.
Now I can say, "Thank you," to everyone today.

Good morning, God; thank you for your mercy.
Now I can say, "Good morning," to everyone today.

Hello, God; thank you for your joy.
Now I can say, "Hello," to everyone today.

Thank you, God, for your help.
Now I can say, "Thank you for your help,"
To everyone today.

Have a nice day, God; thank you for your goodness.
Now I can say, "Have a nice day,"
To everyone today.

Be kind, and share kind words.

Give God the Glory

Give God the glory.
When you are motherless, God will
Become your mother to bless you with food,
Clothes, and shelter.

Give God the glory.
When you are fatherless, God will
Become your father to protect you from all harm.

Give God the glory.
When you come to your crossroad,
God will help you to make the right turn,
Either turn right or turn left.

Always give God the glory when you have challenges
In your life's journey because God will
Never leave you or forsake you.

Step Out in Faith

Step out in faith
When you change your sports team and
You join a new sports team.
You have the faith To know that
Nothing is impossible with God.

Step out in faith
When you change your job.
You have the faith that God will bless you
To become successful in your new job.

Step out in faith
When you move to a new state.
You have the faith in knowing that
God is always with You.

Step out in faith.
God knows what is best for you.

God Paid It All

God paid it all.
When you have paid your last mortgage payment,
Thank God for his love and that God
has helped you to become
The owner of your house.

God paid it all.
When you have paid your last payment on your car,
Thank God for his grace and that God
has helped you to become
The owner of your car.

God paid it all.
When you have paid your last payment for your furniture,
Thank God for his joy and that God has
helped you to have furniture.

All good things come from God.

Showers of Blessings

When you bless someone with food,
God will bless you with food.

When you bless someone with clothes,
God will bless you with clothes.

When you bless someone with a helping hand,
God will bless you with his helping hand.

When you bless someone with your prayers,
God will answer your prayers.

When you bless someone with a house,
God will bless you with a house.

The blessings that you give to someone are the
Same blessings that can become
Showers of blessings for you.

Be a Good Street Sweeper

When you see trash on your street,
Be a good street sweeper; you can
Sweep the trash off your street, in front of
Your house to help keep your
Neighborhood clean.

When you see leaves on your street,
Be a good street sweeper; you can sweep
The leaves off your street, in front of your house
To help keep your neighborhood clean.

When you see small tree branches on your street,
Be a good street sweeper; you can sweep the
Small tree branches off your street, in front of your
House to help keep your neighborhood clean.

Be a good street sweeper; you can help keep
Your neighborhood clean.

Be a Good Trash Collector

When you see trash, either on your steps or
Your neighbor's steps,
Be a good trash collector; you can share love
By collecting trash off both steps so that
You can help keep your neighborhood clean.

When you see trash, either on your lawn or
Your neighbor's lawn,
Be a good trash collector; you can share kindness
By picking up trash off both lawns so that
You can help keep your neighborhood clean.

You can share love and kindness with your neighbors
When you help keep your neighborhood clean.
Be a good trash collector.

When You Share Flowers with Your Neighbors

When you share flowers with your neighbors,
You share the joy of the sweet smell of the fresh
Flowers that you grow in your flower garden.

When you share flowers with your neighbors,
You share love of the beautiful colors of
Fresh flowers that you grow in your flower garden.

When you share flowers with your neighbors,
You share peace to know that God cares
About you and your neighbors.

When you share flowers with your neighbors,
You are not only sharing flowers.
You are sharing joy and love with your neighbors.

Share flowers with your neighbors
Because good neighbors are your
Good friends.

Think, Talk, and Act Positive

When you think positive,
You will have the faith to know that
God will bless you with positive ideas because
You can use your positive ideas to help build
A stronger community.

When you talk positive,
You will have love to know that
God will bless you with positive words.
You can use your positive words to help
Build a stronger community.

When you act positive,
You will have joy to know that
God will bless you with strength—provided that
You can use your strength to help build
A stronger community.

Think, talk, and act positive toward
building a stronger community.

Think Positive

Think positive
When you need to make a decision on
Whether to advance your education toward
Your college degree or remain at
Your current level of education; you have faith
To know that God will help you to choose
Your right choice.

Think positive
When you need to choose the right money,
Choosing either you can get into debt with loans, or
You can pay with cash in order to
Remain debt-free. Thus You can learn from your
Previous mistakes so that you can
Choose your right choice.

Think Positive so that you can choose
Your right choices.

Talk Positive

Talk positive.
When your friends have challenges in their lives,
You can Encourage them to talk to Jesus in prayer.
Jesus can help them to overcome
Their challenges. Thus you can tell your friends
Jesus loves them, and Jesus can answer their prayers.

Talk positive.
When your friends are jobless,
You can encourage them to talk to Jesus in prayer
Because Jesus is a friend who loves them, and
Jesus can answer their prayers.
You can tell your friends that Jesus is a friend
Who can help them to find jobs.

Talk positive to your friends because you can encourage
Your friends to talk to Jesus in prayer, and
Jesus will answer their prayers.

Act Positive

Act positive.

When you help people who are in need of food,
You can give food with love and kindness.
You have faith that God will supply their food.

Act positive.
When you help people who are in need of clothes,
You can give clothes with joy.
You have the peace to know that God will supply
Their clothes.

Act positive.
When you help people who have sickness,
You can pray to God for the healing of their sicknesses.
You have faith that God will answer your prayers.

Your positive actions are reflections of
The kindness, love, and joy that
You have within yourself.

When Your Faith Has Deep Roots

When your faith has deep roots,
You can have faith that Jesus can keep
You from falling down whenever you walk
On rocky soil.

When your faith has deep roots,
You can have hope that Jesus can keep
You from falling down whenever you walk
On thin ice.

When your faith has deep roots,
You can have joy to know that Jesus can
Bless you because you keep your faith
Deeply rooted in Jesus.

If your faith is deeply rooted in Jesus,
Then Jesus will take care of you.

Share Love in Your Community

When you share love in your community,
You have love and smiles to share with
People on your jobs.

When you share love in your community,
You have love and smiles to share with
People in your churches.

When you share love in your community,
You have love and smiles to share with
People in your post offices.

When you share love in your community,
You have love and smiles to share with
People in your grocery stores.

Share love; you can help build
A stronger community.

Share Hope in Your Community

When you share hope in your community,
You have hope and smiles to share with
People in your banks.

When you share hope in your community,
You have hope and smiles to share with
People in your gyms.

When you share hope in your community,
You have hope and smiles to share with
People in your local parks.

When you share hope in your community,
You have hope and smiles to share with
People in your restaurants.

Share hope; you can help build
A stronger community.

Share Peace in Your Community

When you share peace in your community,
You have peace and smiles to share with
People on your jobs.

When you share peace in your community,
You have peace and smiles to share with
People in your post offices.

When you share peace in your community,
You have peace and smiles to share with
People in your grocery stores.

When you share peace in your community,
You have peace and smiles to share with
People in your gas stations.

Share peace; you can help build
A stronger community.

Share Joy in Your Community

When you share joy in your community,
You share joy and smiles with
People in your jobs.

When you share joy in your community,
You share joy and smiles with
People in your schools.

When you share joy in your community,
You share joy and smiles with
People in your churches.

When you share joy in your community,
You share joy and smiles with
People in your post offices.

Share joy; you can help build
A stronger community.

Share Kindness in Your Community

When you share kindness in your community,
You have kindness and smiles to share with
People in your churches.

When you share kindness in your community,
You have kindness and smiles to share with
People in your barbershops.

When you share kindness in your community,
You have kindness and smiles to share with
People in your beauty salons.

When you share kindness in your community,
You have kindness and smiles to share with
People in your gas stations.

Share kindness; you can help build
A stronger community.

When One Door Closes, Another Door Will Open

When you are not hired for one job,
You can pray and you can have faith
That Jesus will open doors for you.
You can be hired for another job.

When you are not approved for your loan
So that you can buy your new house,
You can pray and you can have faith
To know that Jesus can open doors for you.
You can become approved for your loan
So that you can buy your new house.

You can pray to Jesus because Jesus can
Answer your prayers.

Never give up; Jesus can open doors for you.

We Are All God's Children

When young children learn the experiences
And wisdom from young adults and
Elderly adults, young children can grow
With wisdom.

When young adults learn the experiences
And wisdom from elderly adults,
Young adults can grow with wisdom.

When elderly adults learn new ideas
From young children and young
Adults, elderly adults can grow with wisdom.

We need to share our experiences and
Our new ideas so that we can
Grow with wisdom.

God loves everyone because
We are all God's children.

Our Talents Are Gifts from God

When we sing praises to God,
We can use our voices as gifts from God
Because we can help to build God's kingdom.

When we teach Sunday school lessons
To people, we can use our talents as
Sunday school teachers, who are gifts
From God because we can help
Build God's kingdom.

When we usher at the doors in
Many places of worship, we can
Use our talents as ushers, who are gifts from
God because we can help build
God's kingdom.

Our talents are gifts from God so that
We can use our talents to help
Build God's kingdom.

About the Author

My name is Kathleen Iris Godwin, and I was born on January 26, 1965, in the little town of Dendron, Virginia. It had one traffic light, one post office, one grocery store, and a population of three hundred. I grew up in a church where I was taught to always put God first in my life to become successful. In Dendron, everyone shared kindness, love, joy, hope, and peace with each other. Everyone shared clothes and tools, and chopped wood for our woodstoves. Also, everyone gave a helping hand whenever someone was in need of help. I attended Surry County public schools until the sixth grade, when I moved to Portsmouth, Virginia, where I graduated from Manor High School in 1983.

I give all my glory to God, who is the head of my life. God blessed me with a BS degree in biology in 1988 from Norfolk State University. He also blessed me with a radiologic technologist certificate in 1995. I was able to work with faith in God and love for God as a radiologic technologist from 1991 to 2020, when I retired. God blessed me with my husband, Darryl Godwin Sr., since November 3, 1990. God has blessed us with two children, Ericka Godwin and Darryl Godwin Jr.

My goal in life is to write poems with God's words, so everyone can become inspired and encouraged with words of love, joy, hope, peace, faith, and kindness. Everyone can share these same words with each other in the United States and around the world.